Thank you for choosing this book!

We'd really appreciate it if you could leave an honest review.
To do so simply visit:
www.purplecastlepublishing.com/review

Happy
Easter

I spy with my little eye something beginning with...

It's an
Ant

I spy with my little eye something beginning with...

It's a
Basket

I spy with my little eye something beginning with...

It's a
Chick

I spy with my little eye something beginning with...

It's a

Duck

I spy with my little eye something beginning with...

It's an
Egg

I spy with my little eye something beginning with...

It's a
Flower

I spy with my little eye something beginning with...

I spy with my little eye something beginning with...

H

It's a
Hen

I spy with my little eye something beginning with...

I

It's an
Ice cream

I spy with my little eye something beginning with...

J

It's a
Jar

I spy with my little eye something beginning with...

K

It's a
Kitten

I spy with my little eye something beginning with...

L

It's a
Lamb

I spy with my little eye something beginning with...

It's
Mushrooms

I spy with my little eye something beginning with...

N

It's a
Nest

I spy with my little eye something beginning with...

It's an
Onion

I spy with my little eye something beginning with...

It's a
Puzzle

I spy with my little eye something beginning with...

I spy with my little eye something beginning with...

It's a
Rose

I spy with my little eye something beginning with...

It's the
Sun

I spy with my little eye something beginning with...

T

It's a
Tulip

I spy with my little eye something beginning with...

It's an
Umbrella

I spy with my little eye something beginning with...

V

It's a
Vase

I spy with my little eye something beginning with...

It's a
Watering can

I spy with my little eye something beginning with...

X

I spy with my little eye something beginning with...

Y

It's a
Yarn

I spy with my little eye something beginning with...

Z

It's a
Zucchini